BEFORE YOU BEGIN...

Make sure to download the FREE audio program for this book which comes with your purchase! Just go to

www.slangman.com/audio

then look for your book and enter this code:

E2C1EFW4Q56E

Cinderella

Written by: David Burke
Copy Editor: Julie Bobrick
Illustrated by: "Migs!" Sandoval
Translators: Li Li Peters & Ming Tao
Proofreaders: Lin Zhu & Connie Sun

Copyright © 2017 by David Burke

Email: info@heywordy.com
Website: www.heywordy.com

Hey Wordy! and all related characters and elements are © and trademarks of Hey Wordy, LLC.

Published by Slangman Publishing. Slangman is a registered trademark of David Burke. All rights reserved. Reproduction or translation of any part of this work beyond that permitted by section 107 or 108 of the 1976 United States Copyright Act without the permission of the copyright owner is unlawful. Requests for permission or further information should be addressed to the Permissions Department, Slangman Publishing. This publication is designed to provide accurate and authoritative information in regard to the subject matter covered. The persons, entities and events in this book are fictitious. Any similarities with actual persons or entities, past and present, are purely coincidental.

ISBN13: 978-1-891888-21-2

Printed in the U.S.A.

Meet the Author
David Burke

Creator and star of the children's TV show, *Hey Wordy!*, David Burke has been single-handedly revolutionizing the foreign language-learning movement worldwide.

In addition to being a performer of boundless energy and enthusiasm, David speaks seven languages. A successful author and entrepreneur, he has built a thriving international publishing company featuring over 100 books he has written for teen/adults & children. His books have won publishing awards and have sold more than one million copies. David's Street Speak™ and Biz Speak™ series of books and audio programs are used around the world by government agencies, leading universities and major corporations.

Since age 4, David has been a classically trained pianist and uses his musical gifts to compose and perform original songs for his TV series, *Hey Wordy!* which introduces children to foreign languages and cultures through music, animation, and magical adventures. He has also composed, orchestrated, and performed all the music in the audio programs for each of these books.

David's engaging and charismatic persona became a fixture on broadcast entertainment channels around the world, such as CNN and the BBC. David and his work have been highlighted in many major publications, including The Los Angeles Times, The Chicago Tribune and The Christian Science Monitor.

"This series teaches everyday words that occur in your child's life, as well as terms having to do with politeness, greetings, family & friendship."

David Burke

Chinese vocabulary taught:

buyong keqi = you're welcome
da = big
fangzi = house
gaoxing = happy
huai = mean
jiao = foot
nuhaizi = girl
piaoliang = pretty
qizi = wife
qunzi = dress
shangxin = sad
wangzi = prince
wuye = midnight
wuhui = party
xiezi = shoe
xiexie ni = thank you
yingjun = handsome
zaijian = goodbye

Dedication

The entire "Hey Wordy Magic Morphing Fairy Tales™" series is dedicated to all the children of the world.

It is through their understanding, appreciation, and celebration of our differences that the world will become a better and safer place for us all.

1

nuhaizi
(女孩子)

piaoliang
(漂亮)

fangzi
(房子)

Once upon a time, there lived a poor girl named Cinderella who was very pretty. The **nuhaizi**, who was very **piaoliang**, lived in a small house with her stepmother and two

stepsisters. At times it was difficult for the poor **nuhaizi** to live in such a small **fangzi** with her stepmother and two stepsisters. Why? Because they were

huai
(坏)

jealous that she was so **piaoliang** which is why her stepmother was extra mean to her. But the poor **nuhaizi** never complained about living in a small

fangzi with her stepmother, who was very **huai**, and two stepsisters, even though they forced her to do all the work in the entire **fangzi** day in and day out!

5

One day, a royal invitation arrived at the **fangzi** of the poor **nuhaizi**. The king was throwing a party for the prince. And the **wuhui** was going to be big. The **wuhui**

wuhui (舞會)
da (大)

was going to be *very* **da**! The prince was handsome, not only **yingjun**, but also kind. Every **nuhaizi** in the land was invited to the **wuhui**, so that he could choose a wife.

yingjun
(英俊)

qizi
(妻子)

7

wangzi
(王子)

The king and queen also hoped the prince would find a **qizi** who was truly **piaoliang** both inside and out. The **wangzi** was very excited about his royal **wuhui**!

The night of the **wuhui** for the **wangzi** arrived but Cinderella was very sad. Her stepmother was so **huai**, she wouldn't let her leave the **fanzi** to go to the **wuhui**.

shangxin (傷心)

She was so **shangxin**, she started to cry. She was the only **nuhaizi** not allowed to leave her **fangzi** and get the chance to meet the **wangzi** at the **wuhui** and become his **qizi**.

Suddenly a voice from behind her said, "My dear, I'm your fairy godmother and you'll be able to go to the **wuhui** of the **wangzi** and... you'll be wearing an elegant dress!"

qunzi
(裙子)

11

And with a wave of her wand, Cinderella was now wearing the most elegant **qunzi** imaginable. "Thank you! **Xiexie ni**!" exclaimed Cinderella. She was now a

Xiexie ni
(謝謝你)

nuhaizi who was truly **piaoliang**, wearing an elegant **qunzi**, and eager to leave her **fangzi** to meet the **wangzi** at the **wuhui**, and maybe, just maybe become his **qizi**.

13

wuye (午夜)

"One moment!" the fairy godmother added. "Make sure to leave the **wuhui** by midnight because your **qunzi** will change back to the way it was!"

Cinderella thought for a moment and then said, "I'll remember to leave before **wuye**." So the **nuhaizi**, who was very **piaoliang**, left for the **wuhui**. She was

15

gaoxing
(高兴)

no longer **shangxin**, but very happy to be meeting the **wangzi**. As she got out of her carriage, she could hear the **wuhui** and indeed it was **da**! Cinderella walked in

and wasn't too **gaoxing** to see more than one **nuhaizi** waiting to meet the **wangzi**. But after a moment, she calmed down and was ready to

meet the **wangzi** face to face. And indeed he was very **yingjun**! She couldn't believe her eyes! And clearly the **wangzi** never saw a **nuhaizi** more **piaoliang** in his life!

"**Xiexie ni** very much for inviting me to your **wuhui**," said Cinderella. "You're welcome! **Buyong keqi**!" said the **wangzi**. Cinderella and the **wangzi**

Buyong keqi (不用客氣)

danced and danced for hours, until the stroke of **wuye** was finally upon them which the **nuhaizi** had completely forgotten about! Poof! Her **qunzi** vanished!

"Goodbye!" shouted Cinderella. "**Zaijian**! And **xiexie ni** for inviting me!" "**Buyong keqi**," responded the **wangzi**. And Cinderella ran back to her **fangzi**.

Zaijian
(再见)

21

xiezi
(鞋子)

The only thing she left behind was a glass shoe. The **wangzi** was extremely **shangxin** and went from town to town looking for a **nuhaizi** whose

foot would fit the glass **xiezi**.
After days of eliminating **nuhaizi**
after **nuhaizi**, the **wangzi** was
more **shangxin** than ever, but he

jiao
(腳)

had one more **fangzi** to visit. The **huai** stepmother and stepsisters ran out to try on the glass **xiezi**, but it was no use. He still couldn't find a **jiao** to match the **xiezi**.

The **wangzi** was **shangxin** and about to give up, but at that very moment, he spotted Cinderella. There was something very special about her, aside from being so **piaoliang**.

He just had to see if her **jiao** was the one that could fit the glass **xiezi**. He knelt down in front of the **nuhaizi** and slid the **xiezi** on her **jiao**.

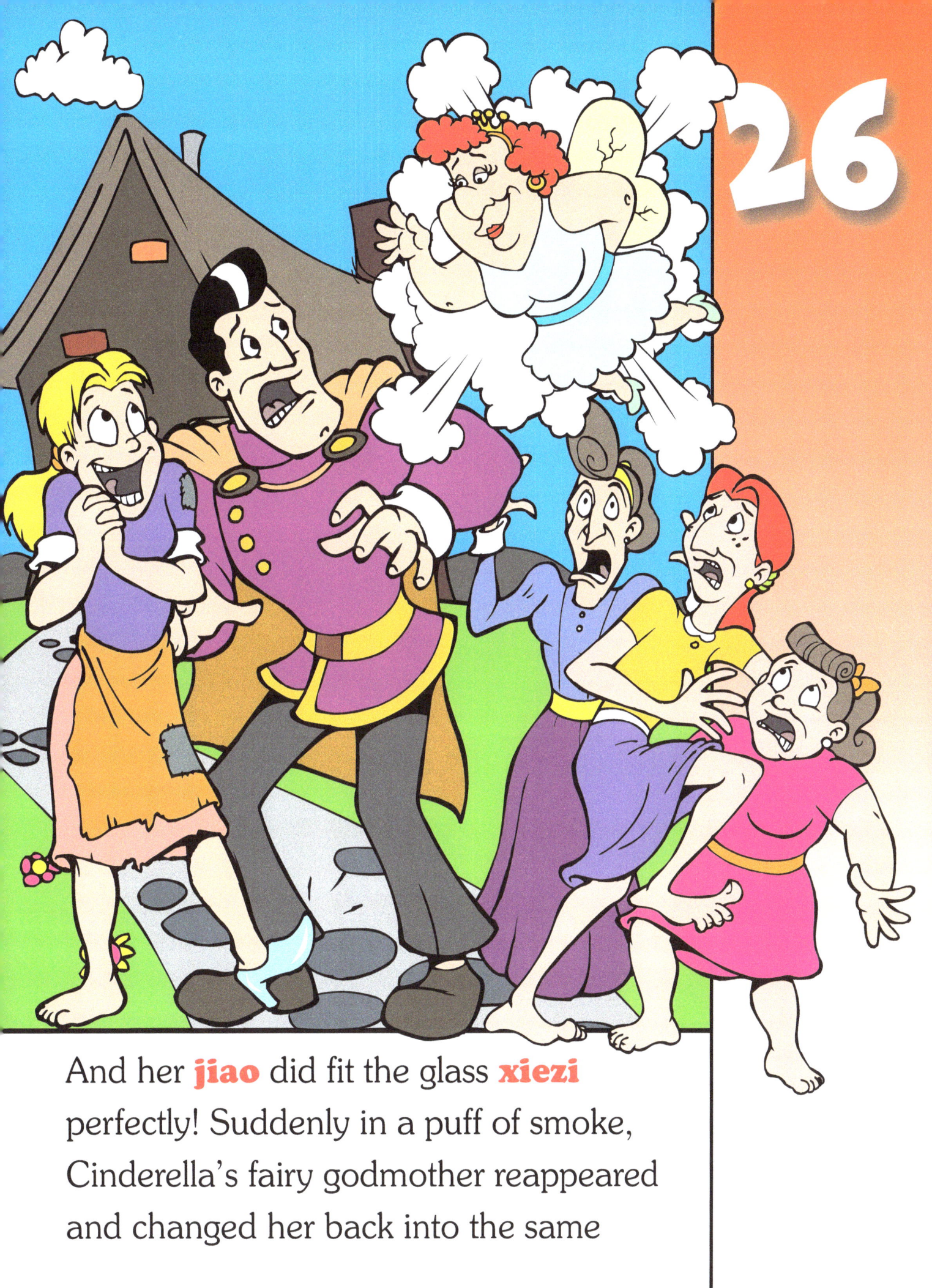

And her **jiao** did fit the glass **xiezi** perfectly! Suddenly in a puff of smoke, Cinderella's fairy godmother reappeared and changed her back into the same

nuhaizi in the elegant **qunzi** the **wangzi** had met at his **wuhui**. The **wangzi** was so very **gaoxing**! And Cinderella was especially **gaoxing** that she lost her glass

xiezi at the **wuhui** or the **wangzi** may never have found her – a **nuhaizi** as **piaoliang** on the inside as on the out! Soon, she became his **qizi** at a wedding that was far from

far from small. In fact, it was truly **da**! She was so very **gaoxing**. She would never, ever be **shangxin** again. And the **wangzi** and Cinderella lived in the castle happily ever after.

Now you're ready for Level 2!

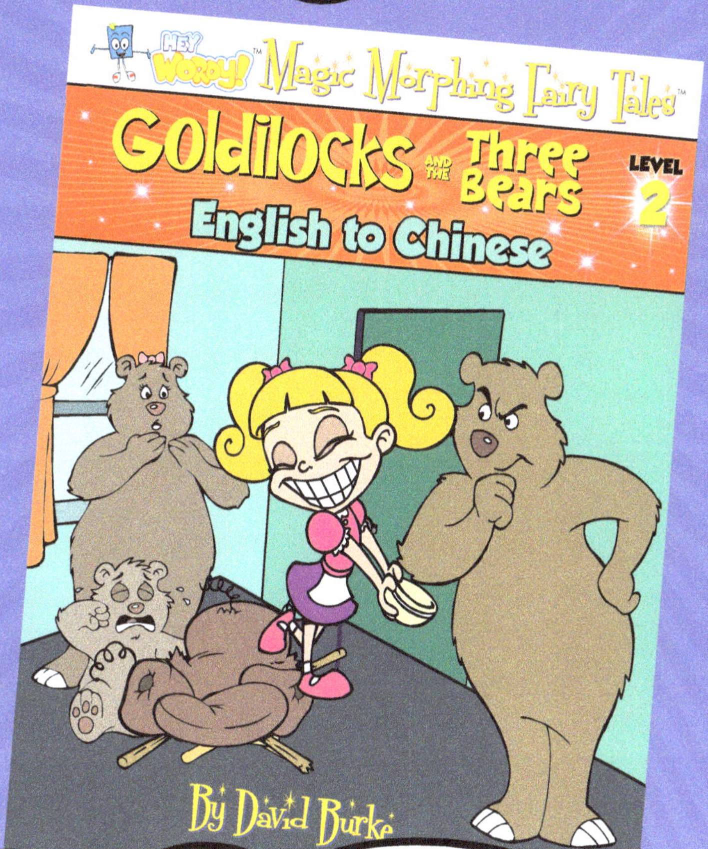

Goldilocks and the Three Bears — English to Chinese — LEVEL 2
By David Burke

Level 2 contains words from Level 1, plus all NEW words!

For more HEY WORDY! products, visit...

www.HEYWORDY!.com

www.ingramcontent.com/pod-product-compliance
Lightning Source LLC
Chambersburg PA
CBHW042031100526
44587CB00029B/4369